GW00715510

30130 121239759

BOWLED OVER

A Play for five women

by

Kay Macaulife

KENYON-DEANE LTD
LONDON, SW11 1TD

BOWLED OVER

A Play for five middle-aged women.

CAST:

STELLA HOLMES	"The Leader". JANE's mother. A widow doing her best to cope with life alone.
KATE HARDING	"The Skipper". JANE's mother-in-law. Rather domineering. A keen sportswoman.
MAY JONES	"Number 2". A down-to-earth person with a sturdy figure.
DORIS MEADOWS	"Number 3". A gentle rather dreamy personality, with a slender figure.
JEAN WILKINS	A Secretary, very business like.

KATE, STELLA, MAY and DORIS are all Members of a Bowling Club, and wear Bowling Outfits.

SCENE: A Sports Pavilion open fronted and facing a Bowling Green. Gate into Club Grounds is off right.
The Pavilion has a door right into toilet and left into Kitchen.
A Pay Phone is attached to wall left.
Seven collapsible chairs and a small table are stacked at back of stage. Various Club Announcements are pinned to walls.

TIME: The present — a summer morning.

BOWLED OVER

STELLA enters through gate and hurries on to stage. She carries a basket with a cake box balanced on top and a handbag. She calls "Coo-ee" as she enters and looks out over Bowling Green. She takes off her hat and hurries round stage, placing hat and handbag on a chair at back. She brings forward a small table and a chair and places basket on chair. She places cake box carefully on table and takes out a table cloth which she puts over table. MAY enters through gate and climbs on to stage. She carries a case, a handbag and a bottle of home made wine. She takes off hat and places hat and handbag back stage and puts down case. STELLA takes out an embroidered apron with a cat on it and ties it on.

MAY: Hallo, Stella, we've got a marvellous day for it, haven't we? Many Happies and all that. I've brought you a bottle of my best parsnip, it's got a real kick in it this year. Just the thing to kill off the birthday blues!

(MAY puts bottle on table, STELLA takes a big salad bowl and a bag of salad and puts them on table.)

STELLA: Oh thank you, May, we'll have it with our lunch.

MAY: *(looking at apron.)* I say, that's a snazzy little number, don't tell me — Doris!

STELLA: *(laughing.)* How did you guess! Yes, she sent it round this morning with a card.

MAY: I see you're lunching us in style!

STELLA: Yes, I've made one of my angel cakes and brought a nice bit of steak. *(She takes out paper parcel.)*
All I've got to do is pop it under the grill, and when that's done — so am I! Just think — no more cooking for a whole week — nothing to do but play bowls and enjoy myself. What a wonderful way to celebrate my birthday, and Jane's coming down to see us off and wish us luck so you'll see the baby: Oh May, she's beautiful!

1

(MAY and STELLA each bring a chair forward to table.)

MAY: We'll need all the luck we can get, we're up against some pretty stiff opposition you know.

STELLA: Oh well, win or lose, we'll enjoy ourselves. After all, it's only a game.

MAY: Don't let the Skipper hear you say that! Once she gets on the Green its a matter of life and death to her. The mere sight of Kate on the warpath is enough to put the stoutest hearted bowler off her stroke!

(KATE enters through gate.)

STELLA: Oh look — there she is. I'll just pop the steak under the grill and open the wine. *(She takes paper parcel and bottle to door left.)* I only hope that grill behaves itself its as old as the hills, and as temperamental as a Prima Donna! Shan't be be long.

(STELLA exits. KATE comes on to stage. She carries a case, handbag and wrapped parcel. She puts case down and places hat and handbag back stage as dialogue continues.)

MAY: Hallo Skip! Feeling fit and full of beans.

KATE: Of course, how about you?

MAY: I've been getting into training in the garden. *(She flexes her right arm.)* Feel that, all bone and muscle that is. There's nothing like a bit of digging to get a bowler fighting fit.

KATE: Where's Stella?

MAY: Taking a look at the lunch, one good blow out to put more power into our elbows!

KATE: We can't afford to overeat before a Tournament as important as this one. I want to fit in a last practice before we go.

MAY: Have a heart, Skip, the Tournament doesn't start until tomorrow, and its only one of Stella's super angel cakes and some steak, and a bottle of my best parsnip to give us a bit of Dutch courage.

KATE: We'll go easy on that. Sensible diet is just as important as skill to a Sportswoman. Remember our Club Match — Jean Davis ate something that disagreed with her and she was running on and off the Green like a jack-in-the-box. She lost her place in my team that day, I'd never rely on a bowler who put her stomach before her bowls.

MAY: Jolly lucky for me she did. I've got her place, and I mean to keep it.

(STELLA enters, KATE kisses her and hands parcel.)

KATE: Hallo, Stella, Happy Birthday. I hope you'll like this.
(STELLA unwraps framed photograph of a young couple with a baby.)

STELLA: Oh Kate — it's lovely — our first grand child. *(She puts photograph on table.)* Look May, isn't she a little beauty!

MAY: Your two kids have got it made if you ask me. Two doting Grand Mothers, built in baby sitters, always on call.

KATE: Not always, May, we're never available on Bowling days. Grand Mothers or not, we've got our own lives to lead.

STELLA: Oh Kate, I'm so looking forward to my first Tournament! To think I didn't know a wood from a green a year ago when Jack died and you bullied me into joining the Club — and here I am — the Leader in a really good team. I hope I don't let you down.

KATE: You'd better not! We all depend on you to place the jack just where it suits us. I tell you we've formed ourselves into a first class team, if we all pull together we can beat the best, and we're going to.

3

MAY: I can't understand why Doris does so well. Delicate embroidery and fussing over cats is more her line than knocking heavy balls about.

KATE: Doris is a very skilful player. The way she manages to thread her woods through the jack takes real artistry. She's got a true eye and a delicate touch.

MAY: *(tripping over a case.)* Well she'll have a job threading her way through these cases for a start.

STELLA: Why don't you put them all in the car, then we can get off right after lunch.

KATE: Good idea! Come on May, no point in wasting time we can still get a bit of practice in before we go. *(They pick up cases and move to exit right.)*

MAY: Talk about a slave driver, you never stop do you?

(As they move to exit telephone rings.)

KATE: *(calling back.)* I expect that'll be Jim he said he'd ring to wish us all luck and you a Happy Birthday. *(They exit. STELLA picks up receiver.)*

STELLA: Hallo!............ Mrs. — who?............ I don't think I — Oh, you're my daughter's neighbour and you — what? This is a terrible line............ you've just popped in on her — how kind of you — and found her dying............ oh — crying? I'm sorry I can hardly hear you............ She's what? On her way over, yes I know I was expecting............ You thought you ought to warn me? Warn me about what? She's leaving her husband and coming home for good? But why? What on earth............ WHAT! He didn't............ He couldn't...... not the BABY!............. And then he told her to get out, but............ because he wants to bring his Secretary home? Well, why not, she's a very nice............ He wants to bring her home to stay? Oh well, perhaps she's in trouble............ What! You don't mean, you can't mean *that* sort of trouble and — he's

4

responsible. He can't be......... he'd never......... Hallo!.........
Hallo!......... Oh, we've been cut off! *(She replaces receiver.)*
Oh, this is terrible. I must ring her back perhaps she's still at
Janes. Where's my handbag, perhaps I can catch her. *(She
finds handbag and takes out coins, she dials frantically completely
ignoring the cast who enter. KATE and DORIS are supporting
MAY who is hopping between them.)*

KATE: Don't put it to ground! Don't stand on it! Fetch a chair,
Doris, quickly. *(DORIS fetches a chair and brings it down
right. KATE puts MAY on it and starts to take off her shoe
and stocking.)* Get another chair, Doris.

DORIS: Oh dear, yes, another chair. *(She brings a chair forward
and flops into it.)*

KATE: Not for you — get up at once! *(KATE puts MAY'S foot
on second chair, DORIS hovers uselessly around them.)*
Perhaps there's no serious damage done!

MAY: No serious damage! I'm crippled for life, that's all!
(To DORIS.) You stupid clumsy butterfingers, dropping a
whole set of woods on my foot!

DORIS: I couldn't help it, it was an accident!

MAY: An accident! I bet I haven't got a whole toe left. You're
not fit to hold anything heavier than a knitting needle. Why don't
you take up darts?

DORIS: Oh dear, I've said I'm sorry - -

KATE: *(examining foot.)* It's not too bad, wiggle your toes — go
on, wiggle them. *(She suddenly jabs at foot.)* Can you feel
that?

MAY: *(yelling.)* Ow! Of course I can feel it. What are you
trying to do? Break the rest of them.

KATE: *(getting to her feet.)* Cold water — that's the thing to keep
the swelling down. Stella, we need cold water.

5

STELLA: What? Cold water — look in the loo.

KATE: *(pulling MAY to her feet.)* Well, you're a great help I must say. Take her other side Doris.

DORIS: *(as she does so.)* What's that terrible smell?

MAY: Don't look at me. My feet are as clean and tender as a baby's bottom Well cared for feet are an essential part of a bowler's equipment. Look out! *(She staggers as DORIS turns to look across left.)*

DORIS: Look at all that smoke! Stella! Something's burning!

STELLA: What? Oh, my steak! *(She replaces receiver and runs off left.)*

MAY: Doris! You nearly had me over then. Talk about a broken reed!

DORIS: *(as they move to exit right.)* Well, I'm doing my best. I'm not very strong, you know!

KATE: Oh leave her to me, Doris, I can manage better alone. Fetch a bowl or basin or something to soak her foot in.
(They exit right MAY still complaining. DORIS runs around helplessly.)

DORIS: A bowl or — *(She sees salad bowl and picks it up. She runs off right.)* Here you are — Here you are.

STELLA: *(enters left, wiping her hands on a now filthy apron.)* My steak! It's burnt to a cinder — I've had to open the window, that wretched grill — *(DORIS enters and removes her hat and drops into chair right.)* Oh, Hallo Doris, thank you for my present.

DORIS: I see you've made good use of it.

STELLA: What? Oh, what does it matter?

DORIS: Oh not at all, if you prefer to use it as a dishcloth.

6

STELLA: I'm sorry, Doris, I've just had a terrible shock and —

KATE: *(entering right.)* If she keeps it soaking it may not swell.

STELLA: *(sinking into chair left.)* Oh Kate, I can't believe it — I just can't believe it. I thought they were so happy.

KATE: Who were?

STELLA: Jane and Jim. I thought he loved her.

KATE: Of course he loves her. Do pull yourself together, Stella.

STELLA: Pull myself together?......... Do you know what your precious son is going to do? He's turning Joan out, and the baby too!

KATE: Oh don't be ridiculous, Stella, Jim would never do such a thing.

STELLA: Oh wouldn't he? I tell you Jane's neighbour rang me up just now to warn me. Jane's in a terrible state, she's on her way here now and she's coming home for good.

KATE: Nonsense! They've probably just had a little tiff.

STELLA: A little tiff! I tell you she's leaving him, and I don't blame her, the brute!

KATE: My son is not a brute. He's a model husband, so gentle and considerate.

STELLA: So gentle and considerate that he threw his own baby across the room?

KATE: I expect he just lost his temper and — he did *what*?

STELLA: Threw the baby into the cot and told Jane to get out.

KATE: But why? What happened?

STELLA: Jane fell over the cat and dropped his breakfast on the floor.

DORIS: Oh, poor thing, was she hurt?

7

STELLA: Yes, she cut her lip and loosened a tooth.

DORIS: Oh, the poor little pussy!

STELLA: Not the cat — Jane!

DORIS: Well, it must have been upset. Cats are very sensitive creatures you know, and —

KATE: Oh do shut up, Doris. *(MAY hops on.)* What are *you* doing? Go back in there at once.

MAY: My foot's frozen, I can't feel it.

KATE: Good! Run some fresh water and soak it again. You must be fit for the match.

MAY: I shan't be fit for anything if I get frost bite in my broken toes —

KATE: *(urging her off right.)* We've got to keep soaking it to keep the swelling down.

MAY: *(as she goes.)* — and pneumonia too, probably.

KATE: Now, Stella, do calm down and tell us exactly what happened.

STELLA: He said her breakfasts were never worth eating, and she was a worse cook than her mother, and then he threw the baby into the cot.

KATE: I expect he was hungry. Men always get upset when they're hungry, and I always gave him a very good breakfast.

STELLA: And what do you think Jane gives him — Pussytins?

DORIS: I don't like Pussytins, I always feed my Timmy on Whiskas, eight out of ten owners —

KATE: Will you shut up, Doris!

DORIS: I only —

KATE: Just keep out of this.

8

DORIS: Oh, I'm sorry I'm sure. *(She stalks to back of stage and sits.)*

STELLA: If you're such a marvellous cook, you'd better give Jean Wilkins a few tips.

KATE: What an absurd idea! All she can manage is a cup of coffee and a biscuit.

STELLA: Well, she'll have to do better than that if she's going to live with him.

KATE: Going to — — — ? Have you gone mad!

STELLA: Jim wants Miss Wilkins to go and live with him. He says he loves her.

KATE: *(pacing round the stage.)* Loves her? Loves *Miss Wilkins?*

STELLA: Yes.

KATE: I don't believe it.

DORIS: Jean Wilkins wouldn't go and live with him anyway. She doesn't even like him.

KATE: Of course she likes him, don't be absurd Doris. And he thinks the world of her — as a Secretary, I mean, but not as — oh, it's unthinkable!

DORIS: If you must know he bores her stiff. Always droning on about his wretched cricket matches when he should be dictating . . . . .

STELLA: *(rising and pacing about stage.)* That's been the trouble. Cricket, cricket, cricket, that's all he ever thinks about. Leaving Jane to cope with the baby every week end when he should be at home helping. Jane should never have married him, she had plenty of chances.

KATE: There's nothing wrong with a man being keen on sport, it doesn't mean he's not a good husband. It's better to have a man chasing after a ball than chasing after other women.

9

STELLA: He seems to be good at both. He's made her pregnant.

KATE: *(sinking into a chair.)* Pregnant!

STELLA: He told Jane she is. If you ask me Miss Wilkins is just like all these so called business women. Out to get any man they can get their claws into.

DORIS: Well, thank you very much.

STELLA: I didn't mean you, Doris.

DORIS: Oh yes you did, you meant any single woman. You wives are all the same, can't trust your husbands out of your sight. You think they're so wonderful any woman would grab them.

MAY: *(hobbles on and sits right, putting her shoe and stocking on.)*

DORIS: Well, let me tell you that a lot of us think we're far better off without a man, thank you very much. And if Jean Wilkins is pregnant I expect he raped her. There are just as many men chasing their Secretaries all over the office as there are Secretaries trying to grab their Bosses.

MAY: Good for you, Doris.

KATE: What are you doing in here?

MAY: I'm not staying out there freezing to death any longer. If I get frost bitten I shan't be able to play anyway. And if I can't get my shoe on tomorrow I'll play without shoes at all.

KATE: You can't appear on a bowling green without proper shoes— its unheard of.

MAY: It may be unheard of but I bet its not against the rules. You've got to wear low heels and the right colour and my heels would be low wouldn't they? It's worth a try, all's fair in love and war and in a Tournament it's war all right.

STELLA: Look, I'd like you all to go away when Jane gets here. This is a family matter and we'd like to deal with it alone.

MAY: Oh certainly if I might ring for an ambulance.

KATE: Of course we can't go, we're all packed and ready for the match.

STELLA: I'm sorry, but I'm not going.

KATE: Of course you're going you can't back out now, you're the Leader and we're all depending on you.

STELLA: You'll just have to find another Leader. Jane's depending on me too, and she comes first.
(Crash off stage left. STELLA runs off.)
Oh, whatever's happened now!

DORIS: *(rising.)* And if Jean Wilkins does leave home I can't go either.

KATE: Oh don't be ridiculous, Doris, all this has nothing to do with you.

DORIS: Oh yes, it has. Jean is looking after my Timmy. I'd never trust anyone else. If she goes I'm staying.

KATE: I never heard such nonsense. You can't let us all down for the sake of a cat.

DORIS: My Timmy is just as dependent on me as Jane is on Stella. I'm not deserting him, and that's final.

STELLA: *(entering left.)* That wretched cat that's always hanging about the Club! It got through the window when I opened it. It's dragged my steak all over the floor it's uneatable now. I'd kill that cat if I could catch it.

DORIS: *(picking up handbag.)* That settles it, I'm going home to look after my Timmy.

KATE: Women! You make me sick, all of you. You're all the same, no sense of responsibility. Men don't behave like this, they stick together through thick and thin, you've no team spirit

11

any of you. Look at you! May terrified of getting her feet wet, Doris obsessed with some wretched animal, and as for you, Stella—

STELLA: Well, what about me?

KATE: You're upset of course you are. We've both had a terrible shock, but we can't *do* anything. It never does to interfere between husband and wife, you must leave them to settle their own affairs.

STELLA: We're not on the Bowling Green now, Kate, and you're not the Skipper. This is my problem and I'll do what I think is best. I'm going to stick by Jane, she needs me.

MAY: I think Stella's right. Women ought to stick together, men still hold all the trump cards.

KATE: You keep out of this, it's none of your business.

MAY: Oh, pardon me for living! Thank Heaven I'm not dependent on any man, I'm quite capable of standing on my own feet. *(She rises cautiously.)* At least I was, now I'm not so sure. *(She hobbles down right.)* Come on, Doris, we're not wanted here. *(TELEPHONE rings.)*

STELLA: *(running to phone.)* Oh dear, perhaps that's Jane. Whatever's happened now! Hallo.......... Oh it's you Miss Wilkins......... Mr. Harding wishs to speak to me, Oh does he? No, don't put me through just tell him I never wish to speak to him again, or to you either, Miss Wilkins......... Am I all right? Oh yes, I'm perfectly all right, which is more than can be said for my daughter or her poor baby, but of course, you know all about that, don't you, Miss Wilkins. You — you — Jezebel! *(KATE snatches phone from STELLA.)* Let me speak to her— Miss Wilkins? This is Mrs. Harding. I know your little game— you're just a typical frustrated spinster, couldn't get a man of your own so you're out to get someone's elses. Well, Miss Wilkins, you're not getting my son. He's no fool, you know, he'll soon see through you. He's got a good marriage and a wonderful wife, you haven't got a chance — you'll have to look somewhere else to

find a father for that poor unfortunate baby of yours and it won't
be my son. You, you, scheming hussy you! *(She slams down
phone.)* Oh, I feel much better now! I'm a very tolerant
fair minded woman —

MAY: Not when you're on the Bowling Green you're not.

KATE: *(pacing about.)* But there comes a time when a woman has
to say what she thinks, and I've done it.

STELLA: You certainly have! You've made things ten times
worse. You tell me not to interfere and then you jump in with
both feet.

KATE: I've a right to fight for my son's happiness and I'm going
to do just that.

DORIS: Oh dear, I was afraid something like this might happen.
You know the old saying "Change the name and not the letter,
change for the worse and not the better". That's what Jane did,
didn't she? She's a Howell, and now she's a Harding, and look
what's happened.

KATE: Oh, for goodness sake Doris —
(Telephone rings.)

STELLA: I'll answer that, you've done quite enough harm already.
(She picks up receiver.) Hallo! Oh, it's you Jane, but why
aren't you on your way......... Did I what? Speak to Jim's
Secretary? Yes, I certainly did, and so did Kate......... Yes,
she did say that — yes — and that too!......... Yes, I did call her
a Jezebel, and I will again when I get the chance.........
She's walked out — good — and Jim's furious, splendid, so am I!
Now, just you come straight over here, and......... What?
You're not coming? But your neighbour told me all about it
when she rang just now......... Yes, Mrs. Williams......... You
don't know a Mrs. Williams? Then — who was it rang?.........
A wrong number? Oh, Jane, what a relief, you mean you haven't
got a split lip and......... have I been drinking? Oh course I
haven't but it's all been enough to......... I'll tell you all about

13

it when you get here......... You can't come over? Oh, but you must, It's my birthday and......... Jim wants Miss Wilkins to come to dinner? He would — the brute! Oh no, of course he is'nt is he? I'm a bit confused......... Yes, I do understand dear, yes he would be naturally, and she would be too. Yes dear, of course I'll apologise to him, and to her too, I'll apologise to the baby if you like. Well, I'll see you next week then. Goodbye.

(STELLA replaces receiver, sinks into chair left and bursts into tears.) Oh, my goodness, what have I done? They'll never forgive me, never!

KATE: *(going to her.)* Of course they'll forgive you, everyone makes mistakes, though how you could believe all that rubbish —

STELLA: The line was so bad, and I thought Jane must have told her to ring me here and — —

KATE: Well, anyway, there's no harm done.

STELLA: No harm done! Jim's furious with me and Miss Wilkins has walked out and Jane's not coming for my birthday, and —

KATE: Come on, Stella, pull yourself together things might be a lot worse. Suppose it had been Jane and Jim. Now, what about opening May's wine and having a little drink to cheer ourselves up, it's no good crying over spilt milk.

STELLA: It's not the milk that's spilt, it's the wine. That wretched cat knocked it over when it got at the steak, and there's broken glass all over the floor. The steak's ruined we've nothing to eat — I'll never forget this birthday as long as I live.

KATE: Of course you will. We'll all be laughing about it in no time.

DORIS: Jean Wilkins won't be laughing after what you said to her.

KATE): Oh my goodness! Miss Wilkins. *(There is a pause.)*
STELLA):

STELLA: Jane said she gave in her notice and walked out. That's why Jane can't come over, she's got to find her and invite her to dinner. Jim wants to persuade her to come back.

14

DORIS: Jean won't go back after all the awful names you called her, and I don't blame her.

KATE: She must go back, Jim will never forgive me if she doesn't. He thinks the world of her, he could never take part in all those mid-week matches he's so keen on if she wasn't there to take charge......... Doris, you're her friend, where will she be?

DORIS: She'll go home.

KATE: Then you must go straight over there and apologise — —

DORIS: <u>Me?</u> Oh no, thank you. All this is nothing to do with me. You keep telling me to keep out of it, and I'm certainly going to. *(She moves to door left.)*

KATE: Doris stop! Where are you going?

DORIS: Into the kitchen when I'm upset I like to clear things up. *(She looks off.)* Oh my goodness what a shambles — the Committee would go mad if they could see it! Give me that apron, Stella — *(STELLA unties apron and hands it to DORIS who puts it on.)* It's up to you to clear up your own mess, and I'll clear up this one. *(She moves to door left and MAY hobbles to door right.)*

KATE: Where are you going?

MAY: To spend a penny, any objections? I've probably got a chill in my bladder so I'll be popping off the Green like a jack-in-the-box tomorrow, and if I do, it'll be all your fault. *(She looks off right as JEAN WILKINS comes through gate.)* There's Jean Wilkins — good luck, you're going to need it, I'm off! *(She exits. JEAN WILKINS enters and strides towards table, she sits very erect and takes out a notebook and pen.)*

JEAN: Now then Mrs. Harding. Your son told me I'd find you here. Perhaps you will be good enough to repeat before witnesses the slanderous remarks you made on the telephone. I'm on my way to my Solicitors, you will pay through the nose for your outrageous accusations. *(She looks at STELLA.)* Both of you!

15

DORIS: I knew they weren't true, Jean, I told them so. You'd never marry him would you?

JEAN: Marry *him*! Not if he was the last man on earth! I have more than enough of him in the office — droning on and on about his footling cricket. He may be a hero on the cricket pitch, but he'll never bowl this maiden over. He's not my type at all, give me a man with brains any time.

KATE: My son is a very clever man, and I resent — —

STELLA: Kate, please! Miss Wilkins this is all my fault. I made a terrible mistake through misunderstanding a telephone call. I'm sure in your business life you must have had trouble with the telephone.

JEAN: As a National Institution the telephone is a public disgrace. Overcharged, undermanned and thoroughly inefficient, but that is no excuse, no excuse at all.

STELLA: I realise that, Miss Wilkins, but Mr. Harding thinks the world of you and if, through my stupidity, he loses your services — the services of the best Secretary he has ever had — it will seriously affect our family relationship. Please, won't you accept my sincere apologies, all this had nothing to do with him.

JEAN: Soft words butter no parsnips, Mrs. Holmes. My character has been most seriously maligned.

KATE: But it was not your character we were discussing. You were in no way involved, surely you can accept our apologies in a sporting spirit.

JEAN: I most certainly will not, Mrs. Harding. The sporting spirit is, in my opinion, a most undesirable quality. It merely encourages people to use any means, fair or foul, to beat their opponents. I am not a Sportswoman and never will be.

DORIS: I knew you'd never leave your home for a man like him, Jean, I told them so.

JEAN: I most certainly would not. Once bitten twice shy, I say — and I've been bitten twice already.

DORIS: Who bit you?

JEAN: I've had two husbands and I'm not looking for a third.

DORIS: You've been married — *twice* — you never told me.

JEAN: Why should I! "Let the dead past bury it's dead" I say.

DORIS: But, you're *Miss* Wilkins, you know you are.

JEAN: And I'm staying that way. "Third time lucky" they say, but I'm not risking it.

STELLA: Weren't you happy in your marriages then?

JEAN: No, I wasn't. My first husband was a Golfer. Even on our honeymoon I was worn out, not by love but by excercise, and so was he — too tired at night to do anything but sleep. Then one day he landed in a bunker and got so furious because he couldn't get out that he dropped dead there and then with a heart attack and I became a golf widow.

KATE: And you married again?

JEAN: I fancied an easy life so I married a business tycoon. There wasn't anything easy about it. I worked like a slave keeping the house immaculate, keeping his books, cooking fancy meals night after night for his business friends and then listening hour after hour to their boring talk. When he wasn't after their money he was chasing their wives. I couldn't trust him out of my sight.

STELLA: What happened to him?

JEAN: He went off with his Secretary, they deserved each other and I was well rid of them both.
(MAY enters and sits right.)
Anyone who married her Boss deserves all she gets we see the worst side of them all.

MAY: You can say that again, I could tell you some tales —

17

KATE: Miss Wilkins, if your husband went off with his Secretary perhaps you can imagine how I felt. My son is happily married with a wonderful wife and a beautiful baby, I was frantic when I telephoned the office.

STELLA: And so was I. Miss Wilkins my daughter is out now searching for you to invite you to dinner tonight. Won't you accept their invitation and at least talk the matter over?

JEAN: Well, I might think about it.........
(STELLA runs off left, followed by DORIS.)
I must say I prefer a man obsessed with running after a ball to one who spends his time chasing after me —

KATE: Then — you'll stay?

STELLA: *(enters with paper parcel.)* Miss Wilkins, please will you take this cake to my daughter, it was to be my birthday cake, but I'd like you all to share it tonight.
(She hands cake box.)

JEAN: Well — that's very kind of you —

STELLA: And here's something for your dear little pussy.
(She hands paper parcel. JEAN takes it doubtfully.)

JEAN: My Fluffy?

STELLA: She sounds such a sweet little thing, Doris has told us all about her It's steak — I had a little accident with it — but I'm sure it wouldn't hurt her.

JEAN: Well, thank you. Fluffy's very partial to steak.

STELLA: It's only for her, Miss Wilkins, not you — you understand?

JEAN: It's very kind of you to think of her, Mrs. Holmes. She can share it with Timmy.

STELLA: Oh no! Timmy mustn't have any!

18

JEAN: Why not?

KATE: Yes, why not, Stella?   Why shouldn't Doris's *cat* have some?

STELLA: Oh, of course, how stupid of me.   I'm sure he'd love it and — er — you will stay, won't you, Miss Wilkins?

JEAN: *(rising.)*   Well — I have got that office just as I like it. "Better the devil you know than the devil you don't" as they say. I'll go round tonight and talk it over with them.   I am due for a rise………

KATE: And I'm sure you'll get it, Miss Wilkins.   Give them our love, won't you and thank you for everything.   Goodbye!

JEAN: *(as she goes.)*   Goodbye!

MAY: Congratulations, Stella.   You've done the trick.

KATE: Stella, you're a genius, there's nothing like a bit of bribery and corruption to sort things out.   Come on, girls the sooner we get out of here the better.
(KATE hands hat to MAY and puts on her own.   They collect their handbags and KATE hands STELLA her hat.)

STELLA: Kate!   I've just thought of something.   Who was that on the phone?   Who has got a cut lip and a loose tooth and an unfaithful husband?

MAY: If she dialled the wrong number you'll never know.

STELLA: But it was Jim we were talking about or was it Kim — she was so indistinct.

MAY: It might have been "him" they all sound alike.

KATE: Well, someone's mother is in for a shock when her daughter arrives on her doorstep but it wont be your doorstep.

STELLA: No, Thank God — Oh, Kate, aren't we lucky?

KATE: We certainly are, if we can get through this and remain friends we can face up to anything.   Now, we've got another battle ahead of us and we're fit to fight it, aren't we?

19

MAY: Well, some of us are.

KATE: Oh, you're going to be all right, I know you are. *(She calls off left.)* Come along, Doris, we're going!

DORIS: *(entering and taking off her apron.)* It's all as neat as a new pin in there. Going? Going where?

KATE: *(handing her her hat.)* To find the best lunch that money can buy. I'm treating you all, we'll toast Stélla's birthday in champagne, pack your things Stella.

STELLA: Where's my salad bowl? *(She packs her belongings in basket.)*

DORIS: Your salad bowl? Oh dear, I think I've put my foot in it again!

MAY: Well, someone has. It's out there!

STELLA: Out there? Whatever for?

DORIS: Well — er — I saw something horrible in it —

MAY: Thanks.

STELLA: What do you mean — something horrible?

DORIS: It got into your salad bowl, so I — I took it out to give it a rinse. I'll get it.
(She runs off left.)
(Telephone rings. STELLA moves to phone, KATE pulls her back.)

STELLA: Oh, my goodness, whatever's happened now?

KATE: No! Don't answer it—you're not here.

(DORIS enters with salad bowl KATE puts it in basket.)

STELLA: Of course I'm here. It may be Jim, I must apologise to him, I promised Jane I would. *(She moves again to phone KATE stops her.)*

20

KATE: No, Stella, it's too soon. Give him time to calm down,
         they'll all feel better about it in a week's time — lets get out of
         here *now*.

STELLA: But I owe him an apology, I owe everyone an apology, you
         know I do.

KATE: He won't be interested in apologies, there's only one thing
         he'll be interested in — the Cup! If we win the Cup he'll
         forgive us anything! And we're going to win — come on, Stella,
         it's up to you now — you're the Leader so lead us on. Come on
         Stella, we're behind you now!

         *(STELLA makes another move to the still ringing phone. The
         others pull her back, KATE hands her the basket. She hesitates,
         squares her shoulders and marches off, they follow her and exit.)*

21